THE ZONE

We would like to also take this opportunity to acknowledge the traditional territories upon which we live and work. In Calgary, Alberta, we acknowledge the Niitsítapi (Blackfoot) and the people of the Treaty 7 region in Southern Alberta, which includes the Siksika, the Piikuni, the Kainai, the Tsuut'ina, and the Stoney Nakoda First Nations, including Chiniki, Bearpaw, and Wesley First Nations. The City of Calgary is also home to Métis Nation of Alberta, Region III. In Victoria, British Columbia, we acknowledge the traditional territories of the Lkwungen (Esquimalt and Songhees), Malahat, Pacheedaht, Scia'new, T'Sou-ke, and W̱SÁNEĆ (Pauquachin, Tsartlip, Tsawout, Tseycum) peoples.

THE ZONE

Rediscovering Our Natural Self

ROB WOOD

RMB

For information on purchasing bulk quantities of this book, or to obtain media excerpts or invite the author to speak at an event, please visit rmbooks.com and select the "Contact" tab.

RMB | Rocky Mountain Books Ltd.
rmbooks.com
@rmbooks
facebook.com/rmbooks

Cataloguing data available from Library and Archives Canada
ISBN 9781771605250 (softcover)
ISBN 9781771605267 (electronic)

Printed and bound in Canada

We acknowledge the financial support of the Government of Canada through the Canada Book Fund and the Canada Council for the Arts, and of the province of British Columbia through the British Columbia Arts Council and the Book Publishing Tax Credit.

Canadä

Canada Council   Conseil des arts
for the Arts   du Canada

BRITISH
COLUMBIA | BRITISH COLUMBIA
ARTS COUNCIL
An Agency of the Province of British Columbia

MIX
Paper from
responsible sources
FSC
www.fsc.org   FSC® C103214

Contents

Wandering bravely o'er peak and sound
adversity embraced, challenge turned around
small self is lost, big self is found
boundless joy revealed and love profound

———

—MAURELLE ISLAND, NOVEMBER 2018

Introduction

MODERN SOCIETY TEACHES US THAT WE LIVE in a world of separate objects, including ourselves. As Alan Watts explains in his book *Nature, Man and Woman*, we learn: "that is a tree," "that is the ground," "that is the sky." This "mechanistic" world view is taken as an accurate reflection of reality.

But contemporary science tells us that water and nutrients from the ground, and carbon dioxide and sunlight from the sky, contribute to the deepest cellular structure of the tree. We can't say for sure where the ground stops and the tree starts, or where the tree stops and the sky starts.

Similarly, we humans ingest oxygen and sunlight from the sky, and water and nutrients from the ground, deep into our cellular structure. We can't say for sure where we stop and our environment starts. It is all one continuous flow of interrelated and interacting energy fields – a very different "holistic" understanding of nature and humans' part in it.

A lifetime living close to nature, researching and reflecting on the meaning of it, has led me to believe that the old, mechanistic world view is missing a critical component that is present in the new, holistic one: the recognition in nature of an intelligent order that unifies the seemingly separate objects of our world, including ourselves. Our intelligence might then be considered part of the whole self-regulating flow of universal intelligence.

Inherent in nature's spontaneous flow is a wisdom that can teach us how to be more alive and more loving. If we know anything of real value, it is how to tune in to that universal intelligence, as do the animals, plants and birds. When we are so present in the moment and attuned to ourselves and our surroundings that we feel at one with them, the universe opens its doors of possibility to us. The wilder and more untamed the vagaries of the environment, the better advised we are to participate in their flow rather than try to control them – to trust their inherent wisdom to guide us through the danger.

Mountain climbers, board riders and other adventure athletes reach the reward for the risk of trusting this deep connectivity: an elevated physical and emotional state we call being in "the Zone." In addition to significantly enhanced physical performance capabilities, including survival ability, this "natural high" induces a profound sense of freedom, happiness and unity with something much larger than our individual selves. It provides a transcendental experience of unconditional love.

Conversely, when we are not in tune with our surroundings and not in the Zone, our natural intelligence can be co-opted by adverse, culturally conditioned notions or mental constructs deeply ingrained in our subconscious minds. Then our perception of reality is severely reduced, limited, distorted and even denied.

For example, the main obstacle to manifesting the unifying power of universal intelligence is the stubborn conventional belief that the human brain is the sole purveyor of intelligence. In my opinion, this is the root cause of most of our problems today, including climate change and a lack of connectivity and love.

The Zone is available, albeit in a softer, more domestic form, in everyday life in constructed human environments, whenever we are relaxed enough to openly and unconditionally engage with the vibrations of our surroundings. This could explain those moments that make life more meaningful and joyful: an infant's smile; a lover's touch; the creation and appreciation of art, music and dance; a cat purring on our lap; a decent conversation or a good belly laugh.

This new book contains detailed reflections on how the Zone has influenced some customs of nature-worshipping cultures of the past and the outcomes of some of my own adventures. It also examines how the Zone is helping me cope with Parkinson's disease. (How ironic that, just as I started writing a book about holding the subconscious mind in obedience and allowing universal intelligence to govern our behaviour, I should be diagnosed with a debilitating disease of the part of the brain that governs subconscious, autonomous muscular activity!) In offering an alternative to material aggrandizement as the primary source of human happiness, I hope it can assist the evolution of the commonwealth of organisms inhabiting our beautiful planet.

Conscious Walking

IN ONE OF MY FIRST ENCOUNTERS WITH HARD evidence of the extraordinary power of attunement to universal intelligence, I watched a friend demonstrate his martial arts skills at our local elementary school. Within minutes, he showed the kids how to be conscious of their presence in this particular place, at this particular moment. Then, by focusing their attention on breathing and their intention on connecting themselves to the ground, they could prevent themselves from being pushed over or lifted off the ground.

I could see right away the performance-enhancing potential of this state of mind for climbing, skiing, chopping firewood – or indeed for any physical activity. It was one of my first encounters with hard evidence of the extraordinary power of attunement to universal intelligence.

Over the years I developed, for both myself and my students, a specific application of being in the Zone: preventing accidents in the mountains through the practice of "conscious walking," coordinating the movement of our arms and legs with the rhythm of our breathing.

When I began to experience symptoms of Parkinson's Disease, the main ones were limping, stooping and not swinging my arms – generally impaired walking. I found that by practising the "conscious walking" technique I had been teaching for so many years, I could walk quite normally. If I coordinated my breathing with the movement of my limbs, exhaling as my injured right foot stepped very carefully on the ground and swinging my arms, I could march like a soldier.

This was very effective for short periods of time but required intense mental effort; I didn't know whether it was sustainable long term. Then, seemingly out of the blue, I received a very surprising email from Grace Gorman, who introduced herself as the daughter of my publisher. She wanted to make a film of my life story – including my mountaineering achievements, my construction and operation of an off-grid homestead, and my work as an environmental activist and teacher – and asked if she could visit our homestead to discuss the idea. I was, of course, excited that there might be sufficient interest among young people, especially in view of my advanced age and physical disabilities, specifically Parkinson's Disease. My only caveat was that the film should include my wife, Laurie, as an equal partner in our story.

Grace was eager to learn more about those disabilities, and she and I both realized, at the same moment, that the film's main story would be enhanced and deepened by the account of my ability to overcome or, at least hold back, the progression of those disabilities by considering them just another challenge, another mountain to climb.

If, Grace asked, there were one last mountain I could climb, where and what would it be? What is my favourite mountain? Through a process of elimination, I chose an 1800-metre peak on the BC mainland coast, not far from our home: Mount van der Est. This would give a beautiful background to the action of the film and provide an adventurous ocean-to-alpine wilderness journey, a showpiece for the rugged beauty and power of the BC Coast Mountain wilderness. The main objective of the expedition was to capture on film my attempt to use my conscious walking technique to alleviate my PD symptoms over an extended length of time and over very rugged terrain.

From our Maurelle Island homestead, we boarded a beautiful converted wooden fishing boat owned by our friend Andy Alsager, a pioneer of long-distance hiking in the Coast Mountains, who would accompany us on the five-day mountain journey.

The three-person film crew hired a helicopter to lift the heavy, expensive camera equipment and give me a boost up to a small cabin in the alpine that served as an advance base camp, while the remainder of the team hiked up old logging roads and a steep trail through old-growth forest. The weather was perfect – if anything, in fact, it was too hot. So next morning we had an early start from the cabin, hiking up easily angled clean granite slabs with sparkling streams running through fissures in the rock and picturesque pools reflecting patches of exquisite alpine shrubs.

I walked in 20-minute shifts with ten-minute breaks; my every movement was filmed. I had to keep my mind from wandering somewhere other than where I was putting my feet. There was no way I could converse, admire the views or otherwise multi-task, so the breaks were welcomed for mental as much as physical relaxation, giving me time to chat and take in the spectacular view down the forested valley, out over the Discovery Archipelago to our Maurelle Island home and the mountains of Vancouver Island's Strathcona Park beyond.

After eight hours of hiking over very rugged ground, we reached camp at the east col of our mountain, below the summit ridge. All at once, just when different groups of participants were separated from one another, we had a surprising deterioration in weather that presented a safety consideration. Overnight, the weather remained threatening; thick clouds around camp made filming and helicopter operation impossible, prompting urgent discussion of our priorities and the consequences of proceeding to the summit. At lunchtime, we decided to take advantage of a brief break in the clouds to count our losses and let the helicopter evacuate us from the mountain so we could regroup in the security and luxury of Andy's boat.

Despite the disappointment of reducing our time on the mountain and not reaching the summit, we had accomplished our main goal: demonstrating how, by being in the Zone, I had held my Parkinson's symptoms in obeisance for a whole day of hiking over rough, trail-less terrain.

A completely unforeseen and interesting layer of the film was its record of the spontaneous and at times intense discussions leading up to the decision to retreat. Sometimes, in the mountains, coming back home to tell the tale requires reading the signs and adapting the plan to suit the changes in the environment.

Self-Discovery

ONE OF THE FEW COMPENSATIONS FOR GETTING old is having lots of time for reflection, research and conversation on the meaning and significance of our youthful experience.

For example, an old climbing friend and myself were recently jostling for the most succinct answer to the ancient question of why we indulged in this perilous pastime that had claimed the lives of so many of our friends. This particular friend, normally a dedicated pragmatist specializing in sarcasm, surprised me with an uncharacteristically romantic and apparently sincere proclamation: "Mountaineering is about self-discovery, old buddy!"

"Great! I'm glad we agree," I replied, playing for time before surprising myself by delivering a sharp response: "So what was it you discovered about yourself from climbing?"

Without a moment's hesitation, as if it were rehearsed, he countered: "I learned I didn't need to be afraid."

"How come?"

"Climbing taught me that by honestly confronting our fears, we can learn to work through them. By engaging reality, we become informed and empowered by it. That makes us feel really good because we feel part of something much bigger than our individual selves."

After a long, thoughtful pause, I summoned the courage to risk his sarcasm and asked, "Does that mean you believe in love?"

Again without a moment's hesitation: "Sure I do! Love is the force of attraction in the universe. It's what is real. That's all there is. The rest is just what we think is real – transitory mental constructs, at best maps of reality, at worst pretentious and dangerous delusions and propaganda."

"Including ourselves?"

"Staying alive in the mountains requires transcendence of ego. Of the illusion of a separate individual self. It requires us to be honest, to get real, rediscover our relationship with the whole universe. Unconditional love."

Hidden Connectivity

I GREW UP IN A PICTURESQUE ENGLISH VILLAGE nestled into the edge of the Yorkshire Moors. Roaming freely for days at a time in the nearby woods, fields and open moors gave me a deep and lasting sense of nature's timeless flow, in which everything made sense and fit together. The village felt as if it belonged in the landscape, and I felt as if I belonged to them both. The villagers' lifestyle probably hadn't changed much in hundreds of years. The milk was still delivered by horse and cart every day, though the first black-and-white TV and the odd motor car had already shown up.

When, at the tender age of 11, I had to leave the beautiful village on the edge of the wild moors and move to the suburbs of a big city, I wept for days.

It seemed that an essential part of myself was left behind. Had I known how true this would turn out to be, I would have wept even longer and harder. My previous freedom to explore the natural world was in sharp contrast to my new constraints at home and especially at the city high school – though, according to my two big brothers and two bigger sisters, I was spoiled and allowed to be rebellious.

At school, I performed just well enough to get by, living for the only enjoyable part – playing rugby. Even better were the exciting weekends away on the fells and crags deep in the remote countryside, sharing rambling adventures and camaraderie with my working-class pals. Ever since early childhood, I have been intuitively responsive to the ability of wild places to affect my state of mind and my emotions. In the old country, much of the landscape was beautiful because it had been "cultivated" for thousands of years by people (and sheep) who were in harmony with nature, but its power was diluted and tamed. The crags where we climbed were more powerful than the surrounding areas because they had not been worked over.

Back in the city, the more I studied urban society, the more it seemed that the contemporary human environment separated people from nature and from each other. Even though I wanted to believe in science and reason, their application to planning and urban management policies invariably seemed to lead to an oppressive, superficial, soulless monoculture that reduced creativity and standard-ized or omitted vital components of life. "Little boxes made of ticky-tacky and they all look just the same," sang Pete Seeger.

Five years' training as an architect did nothing to allay my early doubts about the prevalent cosmology of modern society. It seemed to promote the notion that because we humans are separate and superior, we have the capability and the right to dominate and abuse the rest of the world without any risk to ourselves. This dangerously deluded myth, which inflicted untold damage to the environment and other cultures, thrived on the fact that most of our thinking and behaviour is not actually conscious but rather an automatic replaying of subconscious cultural conditioning (propaganda). We rarely deploy conscious brain power, the very attribute that is supposed to make us separate and superior in the first place. Both as individuals and collectively, we all suffer to varying degrees from delusions of self-importance, which we then impose, often violently, on others.

At least one weekend a month, I would escape the intense intellectual pressure of my studies, not to mention the squalor and hectic pace of low-income life in London, by hitchhiking up to the mountains. The peace and beauty of the remote country offered the perfect antidote – as did the sanity, sincerity and humour of my working-class mates. Stevey Smith, whose house in Windermere, at the heart of the Lake District National Park, had become a favourite meeting place for climbers, became my lifelong friend and fellow adventurer. He shared with me his passion for the authentic traditional folk music of people whose remote rural lifestyle and culture were still grounded in the vernacular of their local environment. After a happy day tramping around the hills and scaring ourselves to death on the crags, we would invariably end up singing our hearts out in a local pub.

Old shepherds sang sheep-shearing and poaching songs with such beautiful harmonies in the choruses that we couldn't help getting caught up in the magical surge of energy, the hidden connectivity that seemed to bind everyone together, transporting us back into ancient times and out into the heart of these mountains and valleys. I had never previously experienced such a profound sense of belonging to something bigger, something I could share with others. I was sure it wasn't just the beer.

Even though these harmonies lasted only a few brief moments, the joie de vivre and energy they generated in that cozy little space lingered on as the landlord shouted, "Last orders please!" well past normal closing time. I knew, then, that I had found something precious, though elusive, a feeling of happiness, freedom and harmony: the Zone. Now that I knew it existed, I would pursue and nurture it for the rest of my life.

Meanwhile we staggered back to our tents, oblivious to the pouring rain, and climbed into our sleeping bags, too tired, tipsy and content to be bothered about the wet. As I listened to the sound of the rain pattering on the tent, I dozed off, humming to myself:

> *I've seen the white hare on the heather,*
> *Seen the curlew fly high overhead,*
> *And sooner than part from the mountains I love,*
> *I think I would rather be dead.*

Wherever we went throughout the remote climbing areas of Britain, we looked for this authentic traditional folk music. But this kind of unself-conscious spontaneous expression was rapidly disappearing, even in the most remote unspoiled areas.

4

Beauty Becomes Love

MY FIRST CONSCIOUS EXPERIENCE OF DEEP, uncompromised wilderness was in 1971, when the famous British climber Doug Scott and I met in a Cairngorm pub and devised a plan to climb clean granite rock walls somewhere far away from societal distractions. We wanted to experience the pure spirit of exploration and self-reliance, free from the bureaucracy, commercialism and crowding of popular places like Yosemite and Banff. We found that isolation in abundance in the mountains on Baffin Island, in the Eastern Canadian Arctic, where magnificent granite peaks, glaciers and treeless tundra bathe in the crystalline clarity of magical arctic light.

After spending six weeks in this pristine landscape with a complete absence of societal noise and clutter, we became increasingly conscious not just of the pretty view but also of a subtle ambient presence, a vibration that interacted and resonated with our feelings and emotions.

We learned that things went better when we paid attention to these feelings and tuned into the surroundings and each other; when we listened and read the natural signs with our bodies/minds open and free. Then, meaningful coincidences (synchronicities) and intuitive hunches happened more frequently, assisting our judgment and critical decisions, especially concerning navigation, timing, weather and avalanches. Conversely, things went badly when we were not paying complete attention to our surroundings and each other; when our minds and spirits were distracted and out of focus. Deep wilderness experience taught us that our well-being and safety depended on conscious awareness of our internal and external environs.

So powerfully did these pristine vibrations affect our emotions that we became hypersensitive about making any permanent impression, guided by the wilderness ethic of "no trace": *Let no one say, and say it to your shame, that all was beauty here until you came.* For instance, we refrained from drilling holes in the rock for protection.

We looked at beauty so long that it became love. We had long periods of being tent-bound in bad weather. Sometimes intensely uncomfortable arguments, soul-searching, confrontation with the demons in our closets... yet we came away the best of friends, having had the experience of a lifetime.

We saw something of the way of life of the Inuit. The fate of their culture is a sad one, but there is still something left that distinguishes them from our modern urban society. The smiles we saw on their faces, especially the kids', even in living conditions most Canadians would call impoverished, are etched deeply on my memory. Their honest, sincere cheerfulness shows a kind of self-confidence and peace of mind so demonstrably lacking in the civilization to the south. They possess an abundance of the genuine vitality that Stevey and I had noticed in remote rural areas of Britain and had come to associate with people whose lifestyle and culture are rooted in their natural environment. How lucky we were to see them with their culture still largely intact. Our brief engagement with the harsh Arctic environment gave us boundless admiration for their courage, tenacity and strength of character.

5.

Pushing the Limits of Possibility

IN THE SUMMER OF '68, IN CAMP 4, THE CLIMBERS'
campground in Yosemite Valley, seemingly quite by
chance, I met an old acquaintance from the Lake
District climbing scene. Mick Burke had a reputation
as a "hard" climber, with several significant ascents in
the Alps and South America. He made it quite clear he
was intending to climb the Nose of El Capitan, which
at that time was surrounded by an aura of impossibility. Only the very best local Yosemite climbers
had succeeded in climbing this, the most famous and
iconic rock climb in the world. The 880-metre vertical
granite wall took five days of supreme physical and
psychological effort in the blazing California sun.

Mick had already made seven false starts with
different partners, all of whom had "psyched out"

and had to "back off," so I was not altogether surprised when I noticed his beady eye focused on me. I had precious little in the way of prerequisites other than being fit and having done many relatively easy climbs. But Mick casually assured me, "It's just a matter of wanting to do it." As an afterthought, he added: "Then just keep going."

The first couple of days, I suffered prolonged and debilitating periods of doubt and fear, but Mick's indomitable and infectious willpower kept us going until the middle of the third day, when he took a 12-metre leader fall. Fortunately I was able to stop his fall, and after a quick cigarette, he just kept right on "keeping going."

Then, in the intense early-afternoon sun, after having negotiated an exhausting series of giant pendulum swings, we passed the point of no return, with all possibility of retreat cut off. Committed as we now were, I remember that third bivouac, on a tiny outward-sloping ledge, as the turning point in my life.

Gone was all the stressful, nagging fear and doubt, replaced by a profound sense of calm and peace. We took the time to look around and absorb the incredible drama and beauty of our situation.

Empowered by this new-found confidence, we completed the rest of the climb without undue difficulty. After five days and four nights of unrelenting verticality, we staggered over the top onto flat ground and were greeted by a crowd of cheering fellow climbers who had hiked up the back, loaded with fresh fruit and beer, to help us celebrate the historic event.

Shortly afterward, I wrote an article about the climb under the title of "Sorcerer's Apprentice," in which I attributed our success to psychological phenomena rather than technical skill and expertise. Mick's ambition and ability to focus his will and positive intention; my allegiance to and bond with a fellow countryman a long way from home; the incredible generosity and support from the local Yosemite climbers; the background aura of love and peace of the California hippie movement at its peak; our awesome respect for El Capitan and the beauty of Yosemite Valley – all conspired to induce a remarkably high degree of synergy that dramatically enhanced our capability.

Proof that we had broken through the psychological "barriers of possibility" that had kept El Cap in the domain of the gods was quickly supplied by the fact that right after our ascent, all kinds of people started doing it. "If those two bozos can do it, so can we": the four-minute-mile phenomenon.

Now, with the benefit of 50 years' hindsight, I can see that pulling the ropes down from the King Swing was like cutting the umbilical cord, thereby casting ourselves off from any possibility of retreat or rescue. The extreme stress of the leader's fall, the King Swing pendulums and the relentless, exhausting exposure to the searing heat triggered the "fight or flight" survival imperative. This fear induced a deep-rooted instinct that puts on hold all body/mind functions extraneous to circumventing the threat, letting us focus entirely on the here and now and dramatically enhancing our physical capability. Most importantly, it also puts on hold the habitual negative subconscious cultural conditioning that tells us, "You can't do this." Once the immediate threat is worked out, the body/mind relaxes back to normal homeostasis and releases endorphins (feel-good painkillers) to compensate for the muscle damage inflicted by the fight or flight.

The unfettered heightened awareness opened our bodies/minds to attunement with the powerful, intelligent vibrations of the mountain environment and the deeper bonding and trust we felt for each other. Relieved of the constant yitter-yatter (Carlos Castaneda's "internal dialogue") of the subconscious mind, our actions were empowered by extra purpose, strength and efficiency. We were doing more with less. The calm confidence we felt during our bivouac at the end of the third day was transformational for me: from then on, I committed my allegiance to the extraordinary power of universal consciousness and the Zone.

6

Not in the Zone

OVER MANY YEARS AS INSTRUCTORS OF WILDER-
ness self-reliance in the Canadian Outdoor
Leadership Training program at Strathcona Park
Lodge, my wife, Laurie, and I have met many young
outdoorsmen. Of all of them, Derek was our favourite apprentice. Still only in his early twenties, with
a burning passion for the mountains and a fully
competent yet modest spirit, he was well on his way
to becoming a certified mountain guide.

It was a fine day in early spring in the Rockies,
and Laurie and I were on a rare visit to Golden from
our home on the BC coast, mainly to see old friends.
We had arranged to meet Derek and his buddy Dan
at the café in Field. He had just come back from an
exciting trip to Europe, and we had quite a bit to

catch up on. Eventually we got around to the secondary purpose of the occasion, doing a bit of ice climbing on the local waterfalls close to the Trans-Canada Highway.

It was late morning by the time we left the café, and although it was sunny on the peaks, the valley bottom was still in the shade and quite cold. We parked by the highway and casually headed up the short hike to the base of Silk Tassel, a modest climb, well within our comfort zone. We were still yakking and didn't expect this little jaunt to take very long or give us much trouble.

Derek set off leading the first pitch, following the obvious weakness up the main concavity of the frozen watercourse. Dan belayed him without an anchor, as was customary for a first pitch off the ground. I set off leading a separate rope a few minutes later, following a slightly steeper line about ten feet to the left.

We had both placed a couple of screws and were about 15 metres up, climbing almost side by side, when suddenly, without warning, all hell broke loose. A horrendous avalanche crashed over us.

For me, it was like lying on the railroad tracks with a freight train passing over me. Because the ice face was steep where I was, and just out of the main funnel of the watercourse, the hideous rush of snow was passing right by and over me. Despite some serious pummelling, I was able to hang on to my axes. My main difficulty was that the rope kept pulling me down. This was because Laurie, belaying me through her stitch plate without an anchor, was being pulled into the pile of debris at the bottom of the climb. With the help of tension on my rope, she managed to prevent herself from being buried.

After it stopped, Laurie lowered me down off my ice screws. There was a huge mound of compacted debris running way out down the hill, but no sign of Derek or Dan.

We assumed they were buried under the mound of debris, so I set off running back to the car for a shovel. Almost immediately, I came across Dan lying face down on the surface of the debris. I cleared his face and was relieved to hear him talking coherently. He suggested I unclip his harness because the rope was pulling him down. I did, after which he was able to move, but his neck was hurting. I was worried another avalanche might come down and suggested he move to a safer spot out to the side of the debris.

I took off down the debris track, following occasional glimpses of the rope, looking for Derek. I soon found his leg sticking vertically up out of the snow. I tried digging with my axe but the snow was like concrete. I called Laurie and rushed down to the car for the shovel. At the highway I hailed a car and asked them to phone for help ASAP. We managed to get him out, but he was unconscious and not breathing, so we desperately started CPR. Eventually a Parks rescue team arrived, but we were not able to save him. He had suffered damage to multiple internal organs.

Dan was taken to Banff Hospital, where he learned he had a broken neck, from which he mercifully recovered. Laurie and I escaped physically unscathed but emotionally wrecked.

I have had a lot of friends killed in the mountains, but never before when I was actually present. Truth is, it shook me up so much that I never did any serious climbing afterward, though I have continued knocking about in the mountains, including some very modest backcountry skiing. I felt guilty and responsible for Derek's death, even as mutual friends insisted that Derek was old enough to make his own decisions, and furthermore that the freedom to take responsibility for your own destiny is a big part of what mountaineering is all about.

One aspect of the incredible challenge of coming to terms with this tragedy was finding satisfactory and meaningful explanations for Derek's parents. They were very gracious and genuinely fascinated about "why?" What was this mysterious passion that had engulfed their son?

The best answer we could come up with was to take them up to Cream Lake, in the heart of Strathcona Park, and spread Derek's ashes in the place he loved the most. There, they experienced first-hand the transformative power of the pristine mountain wilderness.

Another way of coming to terms with the tragedy was figuring out a lesson from our mistakes that Derek would want us to pass on to others. It was easy to say that if we had spent more time gradually engaging with the conditions on the mountain, we would have chosen a different objective. We were in a totally inappropriate state of mind. One minute we were in a warm café full of light-hearted chit-chat, and then, without taking any time or conscious effort to adjust our mindset, we stepped out of the car onto the side of a big mountain with a south-facing bowl thousands of feet above that had been in the sun all morning. Directly below the bowl was the hourglass funnel of the waterfall which, though relatively easy climbing, was serious avalanche terrain. Our minds were still so full of casual and inconsequential social banter that we were oblivious to the danger. We had been travelling through the mountains as spectators, but we'd had no opportunity to feel the vibes or otherwise inform ourselves of the recent history of local conditions. We were not in the Zone.

The essential lesson I learned from and for Derek was that, before going out into avalanche terrain, we should take time to do a reality check on our state of mind. Make sure we are as conscious as we can be of the signs and feedback from the environment and not just relying on automatic, subconscious and probably inappropriate habits. Examine the way the external vibes are affecting our inner feelings and not be shy about sharing and debating them with our friends. Be in the Zone.

7

Collective Zone

JIM BOULDING HAD BEEN A GREAT HUNTING AND fishing guide. But when he discovered what he and his clients enjoyed wasn't killing game so much as the art of stalking (the state of mind of the hunter), he and his wife, Myrna, converted their hunting and fishing lodge into an outdoor education centre. Their well-stated mission was to teach people how to be more in tune with nature.

Jim was a big man with great charisma and a very commanding presence. You could say he had psychic power, with an uncanny shaman-like habit of thinking outside the box, and he encouraged his staff to do likewise. "The school classroom," he said, "was an architectural expression of the box mentality, the root cause of most of the problems of modern society."

Jim demonstrated the joy and power of sharing inspiration gained from interacting with the energy fields of the land in what he called "Generosity of Spirit." When we share the natural high of being in the Zone, the energy feeds on itself synergistically, and amazing things can and do happen.

According to Jim, "There are two types of outdoorsman: whiners and bitchers, and Happy Warriors." I interpreted this to mean we should hold our own subliminal fears in abeyance by being fully focused and grounded in the moment and taking full responsibility for the consequences of our attitudes and behaviour.

Part of that responsibility, which Jim practised to a high degree himself, was what he called "stewardship of the land." Jim and others had been fighting, mostly without success, waves of despoliation of Strathcona through government-sanctioned industrial resource extraction since its inception as a "park" in 1911. In the mid-eighties, the BC government of the day announced plans to open up 25 per cent of BC Parks, including Strathcona, for more mining and logging. This, on top of financial difficulties of running the lodge, became too much, and Jim succumbed to pancreatic cancer. In his final days, I pledged to him that I would do everything I could to continue his opposition.

Fortunately, I was not alone in my pledge of allegiance to Jim and the park. My old friend Stevey Smith and his wife, Marlene, also picked up Jim's baton and vowed to run with it. They too had spent many days hiking in the park and shared his love of the subtle vibrations of the deep wilderness environs. Marlene described that feeling as "having your spiritual batteries charged."

Like David confronting Goliath, we never imagined we could win the battle, but nor could we stand by and watch our mother being raped; we were compelled to do something. So we started a citizen's action organization called "Friends of Strathcona Park," which soon enlisted huge support from the surrounding communities. When "exploratory drilling" started, we organized a permanent camp vigil near the site, even though it was mid-winter, and weather conditions were challenging. On weekends, we formed a human chain around the drill rig, preventing its operation. When the police arrived to remove us, some volunteers refused to leave. They were arrested and taken off to jail. All this drama was captured on live TV over a period of several months, and each time, we had the opportunity to broadcast our message. A Courtenay contingent organized a rally, attended by 600 people, with speakers emphasizing the spiritual, physical and mental health value of wilderness and of clean drinking water. Others spoke to the economic value of tourism. A Campbell River group organized a peaceful sit-in that blocked the highway through the park and temporarily stopped the trucks coming out of the existing mine. This "direct action" attracted the attention of the media, and the event was broadcast on province-wide prime-time TV news. At a huge demonstration on the lawn of the Legislature in Victoria, 50 blue herons circled overhead.

We taught the cameraman how to keep warm and dry, and even he was inspired by being present on the land. That may have come across on the TV, because the sight of all of these decent-looking people being arrested caught the public's imagination, and support for our cause escalated dramatically. Particularly effective in this regard was the sight and sound, as each arrestee was dragged away by the police, of Ruth Masters, a very dignified old lady, playing "O Canada" on her harmonica.

When public opinion polls indicated that as much as 75 per cent of British Columbians wanted their parks protected, the government backed off and withdrew its policy of downgrading BC Parks. The subsequent government increased the amount of parkland in BC from 5 to 13 per cent of the province's total land area, and consolidated in law their protected status.

None of this came about by chance or good luck. It involved a phenomenal amount of hard volunteer work, many sleepless nights, innumerable phone calls, strained family relationships, time away from work – and meetings. Endless meetings. Tremendous sacrifices were made. Decisions were made by consensus, and we used the First Nations method of keeping order by passing a Speaking Stick. To promote and maintain group synergy, we used the Jim Boulding leadership techniques we had honed in the mountains, discerning when to push hard and go for it and when to back off and listen. As the protest escalated, new leaders emerged to help relieve burnout. We received fantastic support from the environmental network and First Nations. One Elder addressing a rally in the park said, "If we destroy our environment, we destroy ourselves."

Through it all, we were unquestionably guided and motivated by the unifying effect of the love we all shared for the land. Those of us who led this rare environmental victory have no hesitation in attributing the success to James Lovelock's "survival imperative of Gaia...the living organism of the Earth and its biosphere" expressing itself through our unconditional love for the park, which then synergistically resonated with the collective consciousness of British Columbians.

8.

Landscape Patterns

IN ONE OF MY EARLIEST MEMORIES OF BEING IN the mountains, I was 10 years old, and my whole family was hiking in late afternoon down a ridge from the summit of Coniston Old Man, one of the most popular hikes in the Lake District National Park. We were supposed to be descending the same route we had come up, when suddenly we were enveloped in clouds. It was no big deal at first; Dad swung into the lead, telling us to just follow him. After a while, however, I noticed that we had gradually moved away from the ridge and were heading down the slope on our right into what I felt quite sure was the wrong valley. When I told Dad I thought we should be heading down with the slope on our left, Dad carried on regardless – he was not in the habit of

9

being told what to do, especially by his youngest kid. It was only when I eventually sat down and started crying and sobbing about not getting back home that night that he finally acquiesced and started pulling us leftward back over the height of land and down into the correct valley.

Now, 65 years later, I see this as an example of intuition, gut feelings, horse sense, the unbiased natural intelligence of a child in the Zone.

....

Decades ago, Laurie and I and eight of our friends embarked on a seven-day ski-mountaineering journey across the Homathko Icefield, deep in the heart of British Columbia's remote and extremely rugged Coast Range wilderness. Homathko is a circular glacial plateau with a radius of approximately 16 kilometres and an average elevation of 2400 metres. Its west half drains into four tributaries of the Homathko River, which flows down into Bute Inlet, and its east half into two tributaries of the Southgate River; its heights of land radiate from the centre like spokes of a wheel.

We had taken a helicopter to a base camp on the edge of the plateau in the Jewakwa watershed, just above a chaotic icefall. From there on, we would encounter no trails, signage or established route descriptions – we would have to be totally self-reliant. Immediately after the chopper left, the weather turned bad and stayed bad, with strong wind and blizzard conditions persisting for most of the rest of the week. Retreat down that icefall would have been problematic to say the least, so we were effectively committed to completing the traverse. Our only technological assistance was a map and compass.

Although the map was accurate and reliable, its scale allowed very little detail of the terrain. The compass was invaluable and effective at providing a straight-line bearing between fixed waypoints, but it did not help with the complex convolutions of our actual course around myriad obstructions. Constant adjustments to the bearings were necessary to compensate for the deviations on the ground. Nor is a compass of any value if you don't know where you are on the map, or if you lose track of or don't recognize the waypoints.

To make up for these shortcomings of conventional (mechanistic) navigation systems, I was able to call into service an additional way of knowing where we are: intuition. Horse sense. Through many years of experience and teaching, I had developed recognition and understanding of recurring geographic patterns in the landscape, which can be used as an additional help in finding the right way to go – a handrail. Even without being able to *see* the terrain very far ahead in the fog, we can *feel* the undulations of ridges and valleys caused by water flowing downhill.

All rivers have catchment or drainage areas referred to as "basins" or "watersheds." All the way around the rim of the basin is a ridge, or height of land, separating it from the neighbouring watersheds. Water flows down, away from the ridges and into streams, in an arterial pattern converging into the main river valley. Big rivers have tributary streams, each with the same pattern at a smaller scale: a secondary catchment area with a secondary height of land separating it from its neighbouring watersheds. These secondary heights of land also converge uphill to connect with the primary ones, which often form the preferred route for long-distance mountain hikes.

The same patterns repeat ad infinitum, like fractals, from the macro down to the micro: patterns within patterns, watersheds within watersheds, all fitting together like pieces of a jigsaw puzzle in which each piece is a reflection of the larger whole. Assuming that we know which watershed we are in when we start out, and so long as we stay in it, we can always find our way home simply by following the flow of the water downstream into our home valley. Extra care must be taken, however, when travelling along heights of land, to keep track of the direction (using a compass) and prevent dropping down into the wrong watershed.

These two navigational aids, mechanistic and holistic, had guided us for four days of poor visibility. The actual physical terrain was not particularly steep, but it was full of potential dangers such as hidden crevasses and avalanche slopes. So, as the navigator, I had settled into a state of continuous amber alert – the Zone – and we were making good progress.

According to the map, the route we wanted to follow would take us along a slightly downward sloping bench below and parallel to the handrail of the height of land between the Hekamie and Southgate watersheds, which at this point formed a sharp ridge that we wanted to avoid. Our calculated bearing, however, was taking us on a slightly upward sloping course. At first I was not worried, as this could quite likely be disguised by micro terrain variables.

As we continued, however, the bearing still took us up slightly upward, and I was increasingly anxious. Something was telling me: "This is not right!" Just as I was about to call a halt, the slope started to flatten out and go slightly downward. Even though this should have indicated we were at last going where we wanted to go, my gut reaction was screaming, "Stop!"

I was inching forward, one step at a time, super-cautious, hyper-alert, totally in the Zone, with my ski poles preventing me from starting to glide. I suddenly saw, between my ski tips, crevasses hundreds of metres below. I turned around and told everyone to back off to a safe flat spot. We needed to get the tents up for shelter from the raging blizzard, have some lunch and a hot brew, and a talk things over.

I explained that we had to figure out where we were before proceeding. Mary had just purchased a GPS, at the time a novelty item that most of us had barely heard of. Once she had figured out how to make it work, she confirmed our location to be atop the ridge. Now we had to figure out the cause of the discrepancy so we could take appropriate remedial measures.

"I think it might be a magnetic anomaly," Mary suggested. Iron ore deposits can pull a compass needle out of alignment. I knew instantly that she was right. That would explain the discrepancy. Furthermore I remembered being here in this general vicinity once before but travelling in the opposite direction: a similar thing had happened, but it had not been so significant because the visibility had been much better.

We quickly retraced our steps and found the correct route sloping down the bench just as the sun came out and revealed everything. The rest of the trip was a breeze down into the valley directly below the mighty northwest face of Bute Mountain, ending with a bushwhack down Galleon Creek back to a warm, welcoming feast from the loggers at Homathko Camp.

....

The holistic order, which embodies energy patterns in the landscape that resonate with deep-rooted survival instincts in our collective memory banks, has been well recognized and documented by almost all human societies other than our own.

Of all the great spiritual traditions of recorded history, Taoism is possibly one of the most in tune with nature. Lao Tzu presented its principles in his classic text the Tao Te Ching approximately two and a half millennia ago. Taoist practitioners consider ch'i energy to be a primordial life force flowing throughout the whole universe, composed of two fundamental elements, yin (female) and yang (male) – not an oppositional duality; more like two mutually supporting sides of the same coin.

The study and arrangement of ch'i in the land is called feng shui. A feng shui practitioner identifies places where the yin energy (lush, vegetated, wet, cold, protected, concave, nurturing, valleys) is balanced and in harmony with yang elements (dry, hot, exposed, protruding, convex, sparsely vegetated, ridges and peaks). This balance allows the ch'i to flow more freely, which is conducive to long-term well-being, safety, peace, serenity, prosperity and survival. The classic properties of such a site are an area of slightly higher ground (yang), such as a small peak or mound, surrounded in the mid-distance by converging valleys with streams and lakes (yin), all surrounded in the far distance by high mountain peaks (yang).

The best examples I've seen, never having been to China, of human-made structures occupying, reflecting and belonging to particularly powerful sites in the landscape (I call them "power spots") are the Tengboche Monastery in Nepal and the Druid stone circle at Castlerigg in the Lake District National Park. What interests me about the stone circle is not so much the mystery of its purpose as the more tangible aspect of how it reflects, augments and maintains perfect harmony with the surrounding landscape. The similarity of these two sites, separated by thousands of miles and thousands of years, is uncanny.

Another interesting phenomenon in rural UK is how many early Christian churches were built on these power spots. Early Christian missionaries were charged by Pope Gregory the Great to build churches on pagan sacred sites. After the site had been selected, the first step would have been to make a plan of underground springs and watercourses so that the masons could design the buildings in compliance with their energy fields. In this way, pagan wisdom, beliefs and traditions – such as nature-worship and divining – were gradually assimilated, co-opted and divested of their original sacred influence and power.

There may be a direct connection between ancient monuments and the presence of underground springs and streams radiating from the precise centre of the site. The involuntary reflex action of the diviner's muscles that move the stick must be due to physical stimuli in some way associated with the presence of water flowing underground. Even though the effect is more likely caused by a discontinuity of or an interference with hidden but powerful forces that cover the surface of the earth, such as gravity and light, it is sometimes referred to as the "Earth Force."

The faculty of perceiving this must have been inherited from remote ancestors, for whom it provided a greater chance of survival. There is ample evidence that fish, birds and land animals use underground watercourses to find their way and to locate suitable places for sleeping and raising their young (horse sense). This would help explain why our remote ancestors set such great importance upon the Earth Force, regarding it as sacred.

In my navigation workshops, I taught people to

recognize power spots by feel as well as by rational analysis, and use them wherever possible for rest and relaxation, as safe places in which to charge our spiritual batteries. Avalanche awareness experts recognize "islands of safety" that coincide with feng shui sites and Druids' sacred sites.

9.

Vision Quest

EVER SINCE COMING TO THE NORTHWEST COAST,
I had been fascinated by the extraordinarily beautiful Indigenous art and artifacts to be found there,
manifestations of one of human history's unique
examples of a society deeply connected and in tune
with nature. Indigenous Peoples of the Northwest
Coast consider themselves participants in the great
circle of creation rather than subjects of an external,
separate creator. External reality is a reflection of
themselves, and vice versa.

Newly arrived on the coast, I was inspired by
the magnificent Indigenous artifacts on display
in the Museum of Anthropology in Vancouver,
from gigantic cedar totem poles to tiny bracelets
and hand-carved insignias. Every item seemed not

only functional but infused with meaningful joy and beauty. It inspired in me a craving for a more authentic experience of culture.

As I was soon to find out, however, evidence of the real living culture was easier to find tucked safely away in various museums of the world than in the original village sites, many of which were abandoned and buried deep in weeds and blackberry bushes, with the artists and artisans living in reservations, demoralized by poverty. This sad state of affairs came about as a direct result of rampant colonialism: the decimation of Indigenous populations by the spreading of TB and smallpox epidemics that could have been prevented; federal laws banning the Potlatch ceremonies; the theft of ceremonial regalia, such as masks; the creation of residential schools that separated children from their parents and levied brutal, shameful punishment upon children for speaking their own languages.

Years later, after I had built a strong, seaworthy boat capable of taking us to the more remote coves and beaches of the coast, I was encouraged to find a cultural renewal happening, with brand new totem poles going up, and renewed artistic expression of deep-rooted unity with nature.

About that same time, the Canadian Outdoor Leadership Training program at Strathcona Park Lodge ran a customized wilderness guides program for young adults from the 'Namgis First Nation. Laurie and I were asked to contribute our usual four-day workshop on wilderness self-reliance. Our job was much easier than usual because it did not take much scratching at the surface to reveal our students' profundity of skills and understanding of the subject material – to the point that the normal teacher–student relationship was somewhat reversed, and we became the students. They may have forgotten or perhaps had never even been shown how to light a fire in the rain, but once the subject was introduced as a legitimate part of the course curriculum, no further explanation of its relevance or methodology was required. Within no time, dry cedar kindling and fir pitch were found, the fire was lit and a circle of makeshift seats was formed around it. The kettle was on for hot drinks; food was cooking, clothes drying and spirits rising. After supper, accompanied by drumming, singing and chanting, they told stories of legendary characters that were part human and part animal, possessed of extraordinary powers, whose personalities echoed their own.

The most memorable part of the trip for me was when all 12 of us were paddling a Voyageur canoe back across Buttle Lake to the lodge. Listening to the drums, with everyone chanting in rhythm with the waves, I had an epiphany. I noticed how, in our wake, gentle ripples on the surface of the calm, sunny water caused the reflections of the spectacular landscape to break up into oval pools of colour surrounded by black and white lines, exactly synonymous with the essential graphic component of West Coast Indigenous art, the ovoid. In art as in life, these ovoids resembled eyes, turning the observer into observed. Through the medium of Indigenous art, I saw myself the same way the artists most likely saw themselves: as inseparable from the landscape.

When we parted, the group's leader presented us with an orca silkscreen print as a token of respect and recognition that we were "people of the whale spirit." It still hangs in our living room, and we hold it in great esteem, its powerful central ovoid looking over us, and looking out for us, every day.

The group also invited us back to Alert Bay to meet with their Elders and discuss a plan for introducing adventure tourism. Since arriving on the coast, I had dreamed of sailing across the Hecate Strait to

Haida Gwaii. And so, one evening in August 1990, our ten-metre catamaran, *Quintano*, quietly slipped her moorage and motored out into the Okisollo rapids with the beginning of the ebb tide.

From the moment we tied up at the government dock at Alert Bay, we received exceptionally friendly hospitality. We were taken to the community's pride and joy, a brand-new, extremely elegant museum that represented both literally and symbolically the recovery of stolen Potlatch regalia, masks, dances and language. Close by, casting a dark shadow, stood a hideous four-storey brick box: the relic of the residential school. We were informed that the community had recently voted, at long last, to demolish it.

Next, we were shown the world's tallest totem pole and another brand-new building that our hosts presented with great pride: the recently rebuilt Big House. The old one had been burned down, apparently by arson; the new one is an exact replica. I was familiar with photographs of stunning architectural elements of this traditional Longhouse, particularly the massive log post-and-beam structure, but those pictures did not replicate the powerful emotional impact of standing inside, experiencing the ambience, being embraced by the all-encompassing harmony, beauty and power of that building. So far I have described the Zone in relation to deep connectivity with the natural environment; here I was witnessing an architectural environment, an aesthetic expression of a whole society, that brought me to the Zone.

Over lunch, we were given the opportunity to answer questions from the Elders on how ecotourism could provide employment for 'Namgis young people and at the same time engage them with the spiritual power of the land. A specific suggestion on the table was to re-establish the traditional Grease Trail trading route across Vancouver Island to connect with neighbouring Indigenous groups.

For thousands of years, Indigenous traders used the well-trodden Grease Trails to transport eulachon oil, a highly valuable commodity. A small sardine-like fish, the eulachon makes annual runs into the rivers of the mainland coast; when it is boiled in a traditional cedar bent box, the edible grease separates and rises to the top. It can then be skimmed and stored for many months. Grease Trails often went over the Coast Mountains to the Interior, but the 'Namgis also had one across the Vancouver Island mountains to their neighbours on the West

Coast, who had no grease of their own because the eulachon only ran up the mainland rivers. These trails were also used for social connectivity, such as intermarriage of Chiefs.

For the 'Namgis Nation, reopening the Grease Trail to Yuquot, also known as Friendly Cove, would have highly symbolic importance for the revival of their language and culture. Our specific suggestion was that they develop an eight-day ocean-to-alpine wilderness adventure. Starting out from Alert Bay, participants could paddle up the Nimpkish River, hike over the divide down to Tahsis and kayak down to Yuquot on Nootka Island, encountering as much Indigenous culture as possible along the way. All of which could fit into a two-week holiday package tour from Europe to the airport in Campbell River and back. We considered it a great honour to accept the invitation to be part of the endeavour.

After leaving Alert Bay, we continued sailing up to the northern end of Vancouver Island and the last sheltered anchorage before 50 kilometres of exposed ocean to Cape Caution and another 15 kilometres to regain the relative shelter of the Inside Passage behind Calvert Island. This time, we had a new formidable element to contend with: thick fog.

Quintano motored timidly out of the narrow harbour mouth and clung closely against the shore; we peered into the featureless grey gloom. Visibility was just enough to keep us clear of the rocks. It did not take long, even at slow speed, to reach the lighthouse at the northern end of Vancouver Island, with its eerie foghorn and ghostly light.

This was the point of no return. A decision had to be made: proceed with our plan to head north, or turn and head back home. Continuing north would mean leaving the sheltered anchorage and heading out into the open ocean – an ocean of fog. We had no GPS or Chartplotter. We trusted the compass and had experience dealing with fog on the inside coast, but we had never been out in the open ocean in fog.

Frankly, I was scared of that damn fog. I felt nauseous with indecision and fear; I knew I was wimping out. As we turned around, I tried to rationalize by muttering, "Let's try again tomorrow."

We were once again trying to pick out the rocky shore from the impenetrable grey gloom when Kiersten, our lookout on the bow, shouted: "Look! Look! A whale!"

A huge grey whale gently broke the surface halfway between *Quintano* and the rocks. As if to confirm its presence – which we could have been excused for doubting, given the perfect camouflage of its grey barnacled back against the grey swell, grey rocks and grey fog – it let out, with a snort, a spout of vapour before rolling forward into the swells. Spellbound, we eagerly anticipated its rising for a repeat performance. It soon obliged, this time even closer, exposing even more of its body and tail. We gasped as, almost right alongside *Quintano*, it turned its head, showing us a doleful and compassionate eye. I could have sworn it was smiling, even winking.

"Look! Look! There's another one, two, three!" yelled Kiersten. At least half a dozen grey whales appeared all around us. I instinctively turned the helm to follow them back the way we had just come, toward the open sea. Entertained by this playful exhibition of hide-and-go-seek by the whales, we switched the engine off so we could better hear their blowing and the swishing of their flukes. They were not at all threatening, even though at times they were only a few feet away from the boat.

As the novelty of watching the whales wore off, I started the motor and locked my focus onto the compass bearing: 340 degrees, 20 sea miles to Pine Island, another ten to Cape Caution. I opened the throttle, and *Quintano*'s bows cut smoothly into the ocean swell. Before I had a chance for further reflection or doubt, we had lost sight of land and the whales and were out in the open Pacific.

From there we made good progress, keeping on schedule up the Inside Passage to Gillen Harbour, the last haven on the mainland side before the jumping-off point for the crossing of the infamous Hecate Strait. What amateur sailor in a homemade boat would not be intimidated by the prospect of sailing across one of the roughest stretches of ocean on the planet?

Having made good progress so far, and with a favourable forecast of 20-to-25-knot northwesterly wind, we were reasonably confident. We had been advised that the seas would be worse on the mainland side because of strong tidal currents and more exposure to the big ocean swell coming from the southwest. Early next morning, however, as we rounded the point at the mouth of Gillen Harbour, we were shocked by how chaotic the waves were, even though the wind itself was not severe. With a modest amount of sail, just a single jib, we settled into a course due west on a beam reach across the northerly wind. The most uncomfortable part was the violent slap of the surface chop against the windward side of the hull, which sent great dollops of green water directly up in the air and then right down on top of the helmsman.

After two hours' sailing, just before we lost sight of the land, we took compass bearings to get a fix on our position. We figured that we would decide whether or not to turn back based on how far we had come. To our surprise and satisfaction, we had already travelled 40 kilometres at an average speed of 12 knots. We were already one-third of the way along our 120-kilometre crossing. This excellent progress encouraged us to keep going. Soon we could make out the skyline of the Haida Gwaii mountains, the seas mellowed out, and we continued to make good, comfortable progress all the way into the sheltered anchorage of Windy Bay on Haida Gwaii, having completed the crossing in ten hours at an average speed of 10 knots with just a single jib.

A few other sailboats were anchored in the bay. Our shallow draft allowed us to anchor closer to the beach than the others, knowing that when the tide went out in the morning, *Quintano* would be sitting high and dry.

After a good sleep-in, I stepped off the boat onto the beach to check things out. I noticed an elderly fellow casually approaching, and after a friendly welcome, he was curious as to how we had managed to get so much closer into the shore than any other sailboat of our size he had ever seen before. I explained two of the advantages of catamarans: their shallow draft, and their ability to sit the two hulls down on a beach.

After a very long pause, he asked, "So you got two boats then, eh?"

"That's right!"

After another long pause: "Do you sleep in them or just storage?"

"Just storage."

With a wry chuckle, he suggested, "So you got your pop on one side and your chips on the other, eh?"

We cracked up laughing and shook hands. He invited us up for coffee at his cabin, tucked away in the forest just above the high tide. He introduced himself as Wes and his wife as Bubby and explained that they were Haida Elders. They were the official Watch Keepers over this historic site, where, in 1985, 72 Haida warriors had taken a stand against clear-cut logging of the magnificent old-growth forest of their homeland.

This courageous act of non-violent civil disobedience was shown on TV, with dramatic images of Haida Elders, many of them women, dressed in their traditional black-and-red gowns and elegant conical hats, beating their drums against a backdrop of pristine forest on one side and bulldozers on the other. The spectacle of these Elders being taken away by the RCMP caught the public's imagination; widespread support for the Haida eventually led to the allocation of the whole of South Moresby as a national park. Part of the negotiation between Haida Gwaii and Parks Canada was that the park should create alternative employment opportunities for Haida people, such as Watch Keeping.

Our last port of call before leaving Haida Gwaii was the village of Ninstints, located on SGang Gwaay, a small, remote island off the southwest coast. Now a World Heritage Site, the village has been allowed, in the Haida tradition, to decay naturally, returning to the land from which it was fashioned. In addition to the remains of cedar Longhouses, Ninstints features carved mortuary and memorial poles recognized as some of the finest of their kind, representing the world's largest gathering of totem poles still in their original location.

With the village no longer inhabited, I had to resist the temptation to feel mournful; I tried to imagine what it must have been like there with the houses spread out along the shoreline, each with a beautifully carved cedar canoe pulled up on the beach, with all the poles still standing. Then I realized how profoundly lucky we were to witness this evidence of the inhabitants' connectivity with nature, and their acceptance of its inherent cycles of growth and decay. Unlike other civilizations, including ours, this one did not need to create lasting monuments to itself, as if it were separate from or superior to its environment.

Quintano ran like a horse heading for the barn, sailing back down Johnstone Strait with spectacular speed and perhaps the most exhilarating sailing of the whole trip. As well as the normal satisfaction of getting where we wanted to go by using the wind without diminishing it, there was the additional thrill of riding a dynamic balance between speed and safety. The mechanical efficiency of this process is fine-tuned: one hand, on the tiller, responds to the sideways heeling thrust on the sails (safety); the other, on the main sheets, controls the tension and shape of the sails (speed). This intense participation in the flow of events, in the interaction between ocean, wind, boat and sailor, brings the rhythm of your thoughts and actions into harmony and unity with the natural environment – the Zone. Catamarans are particularly sensitive, having no limit to their hull speed or their ability to capsize, which is even more demanding on the concentration and skill of the helmsperson, and even more exciting and rewarding.

We completed the 1300-kilometre journey in just ten days. We arrived home just in time to rescue one of our pigs, which had broken loose from the pen and was harassing our neighbours. Thanks largely to *Quintano*'s strength of character, Laurie and I survived a wonderfully exciting adventure which, in the calmer light of retrospect, was one of the highlights of our lives and left us with a warm, euphoric glow. The memory of *Quintano* surging through the ocean swells; of communicating with the grey whales; of crossing Hecate Strait; of the majesty of Haida totem poles on sᴳᴀɴɢ Gwaay and the 'Namgis ceremony in the Big House at Alert Bay – these will stay with us forever.

Did the whales tell us it was okay to proceed? I believe, at least, that our attention being focused on the whales connected us with their natural universal intelligence, which in turn took us out of the subconsciously conditioned box of fear and doubt that had prevented us from proceeding.

10.

Journey into Science

AS EARLY AS MY TEENAGE ROCK CLIMBING AND mountaineering adventures, I had inexplicable feelings of hidden connectivity, freedom and joy that led to an intense curiosity about the age-old question: Why do we climb mountains? It was easy to brush the question off by saying "because it is fun" or "because it is there," but that was to deny the deeper mystery. To the vast majority of people who have never had the experience, anyone who deliberately risks their own life must seem crazy. I soon learned that any explanation of that mystery would require a fundamentally different understanding of reality.

Five years' training as an architect did nothing to allay my early doubts about the veracity of the prevalent world view of modern society. Even though I wanted to believe in science, logic, objectivity and reason, their application to planning and urban management policies invariably seemed to lead to a standardized monoculture that omitted vital components of life. This presented another profound question: What exactly was it that I found to be so fundamentally wrong or missing in contemporary society? Answering that, too, would require a different world view.

Answering these two questions became a lifetime intellectual quest. I had an intuitive hunch that answering either of them would also answer the other. I knew society considered climbers insane, but I was not at all sure it wasn't society that was insane.

I was interested in any subject that might shed light on or explain my beyond-"normal" experiences in mountains and wild places. Although I was fascinated by Eastern religious philosophy, I was more inclined to be convinced, if possible, by scientific proof.

From the sprinkling of general science in my high school education, I knew that, in any interaction of two energy fields, when the frequency of each field's wave is in sync or in tune with the other's, they resonate and harmonize to produce a new wave of higher amplitude ("constructive interference"). When the frequencies are out of sync, they cancel each other out ("destructive interference").

The balance of the whole universal system is maintained by a self-regulating process in which the outcome of any energy transformation feeds back, through harmonic resonance, to enhance the original source. This harmonic convergence constitutes the intelligent and harmonious order of nature that we see and feel around and within us.

The possibility of a new holistic science that might explain my experience of "extraordinary" or "paranormal" reality took a quantum leap when I read Fritjof Capra's 1975 book *The Tao of Physics*. It explains how, at the start of the twentieth century, a fundamental disagreement existed in physics as to whether light was made of particles or waves. The famous two-slit experiment of quantum physics showed not only that it was potentially both but also that the particles were choosing which aspect of themselves (particle or wave) would materialize at any particular moment, depending, among other things, on whether or not they were being observed. Subatomic particles *knew* instantly, over vast distances, what each other was doing and behaved differently when observed or measured.

This radical notion, now referred to as "non-locality" – that when we observe reality, we change it, and that matter can be affected by "mind" – posed irreconcilable challenges to the conventional mechanistic world view. Because instant connectivity implied something travelling faster than the speed of light, which Einstein claimed was impossible, he called it "spooky action at a distance."

A generation later, the eminent quantum physicist David Bohm reconciled Einstein's problem with quantum theory by suggesting that instant connectivity did not necessarily require a message moving faster than the speed of light, because our observation and/or measurement of the event caused the particles to manifest an instant quantum leap into the "wave aspect" of their relationship. In his book *Wholeness and the Implicate Order*, Bohm presents his vision of "the universe as being one undivided wholeness like a hologram, any part of which contains and is a reflection of the whole." According to Bohm, in the particle/wave duality, the "particle aspect" is manifest in the familiar mechanistic world view of visible, separate individual objects, while the invisible "wave aspect" is inherently "enfolded" within a background field of potential relationship, which he called the "implicate order." Just as easily, the wave aspect can unfold out of the implicate order into individual material form within the "explicate order" of familiar, everyday mechanistic reality.

"The implicate order," Bohm writes, "is the immediate and primary actuality in which consciousness is no longer considered to be fundamentally separate from matter. If matter and consciousness could in this way be understood together...we could come to the germ of a new notion of unbroken wholeness, in which consciousness is no longer to be fundamentally separated from matter."

In her book *The Quantum Self*, renowned physicist Danah Zohar explains that when subatomic particles interfere with each other, the higher-energy harmonic convergence of the wave function of their relationships spreads instantaneously and indeterminately throughout the background field of potential possibilities. The wave aspects of electrons can overlap and "merge" so that their "inner qualities... become indistinguishable from the relationship among them." Comparing these electrons to birds or fish that can suddenly change direction en masse without colliding, Zohar suggests that this relationship, which has been called "relational holism," may be the origin and meaning of consciousness.

My own understanding, gleaned from various sources, is that human brains, like radio and TV sets, receive a multitude of signals (electromagnetic vibrations) broadcast in the environment, and select (tune into) the frequency of the preferred channel, interpreting the signals and instructing the body cells to deliver the appropriate behavioural response. Our senses have evolved to help us survive by perceiving and adapting to changes in our environment.

When the frequency of the flow of our behavioural response feeds back and resonates in harmonic convergence (constructive interference) with that of the original message from the external environment, we feel the fluctuating balance and participate in a symbiotic relationship with it (like a kid learning to ride a bike, or a surfer the wave). Being in the Zone is potentially, then, much more than simply being fully present in the moment with open-minded awareness ("mindfulness") of changes in the environment: it can also be an opportunity to participate in creating those changes. It seems to me that we have the choice of whether to do so constructively (connectivity) or destructively (separation). But making the right choice is not always easy, because the subconscious mind can be devious and easily manipulated by social conditioning.

Evolution of the human brain allowed us not only to rely on instinctual behaviour traits inherited in our genes but also to learn from the life experience of other people: parents, community, society. This social conditioning allows repeated, predictable signals in the environment to elicit standard, learned (conditioned) responses, which are then stored in the subconscious memory bank and passed on to the next generation. Through repeated successful application, these standard behavioural responses (traits) become automatic, habitual, programmed mindsets – for example, driving a car.

Appropriate social conditioning provides an evolutionary advantage because it leaves the conscious mind free to observe and evaluate unfamiliar signals from an ever-changing external environment. But what happens if and when the teachers' perceptions of reality are inaccurate, obsolete, purposefully contorted or just plain wrong? We are lumbered with default limited perception (Huxley's "reducing valve") and impaired understanding of reality: tunnel vision.

Fortunately, the conscious mind has the capacity to override the subconscious mind's preprogrammed default behaviour and determine whether the habitual response is appropriate or not. If not, it can adapt the behavioural response accordingly. That conscious intention is a fundamental survival imperative both for climbers in the mountains and, I suspect, for human societies. It is also the foundation of free will – the realization of which is being in the Zone.

....

My layperson's humble understanding of these scientific principles, which are consistent with my experience, suggests that the critical component of reality missing from the old, mechanistic world view but present in the new, holistic one is the recognition of nature's intelligent order (mind), which unifies the seemingly separate objects of our world, including ourselves. It is one of the most deeply held tenets of the mechanistic world view that intelligence is the sole prerogative of the human brain. In the new, holistic view, our intelligence is considered part of the whole of universal intelligence. It exists, like magnetism, in a mind field that permeates all matter in the whole universe, including inanimate matter, such as rocks and mountains, as well as the deepest cellular structure of our human bodies/minds.

Being in the Zone is not, then, the addition of some mysterious sixth sense so much as a breaking free from the heavy constraints of inappropriate, culturally conditioned thinking that prevents accurate perception of and appropriate response to the natural, spontaneous flow of universal intelligence, which can teach us how to live more sustainably and be more alive, conscious and loving.

Insofar as we *know* anything of real value, it is how to engage and tune into universal intelligence as do the animals, plants and birds. Migrating birds, salmon and other animals *know* their way home; some dogs reportedly *know* when earthquakes and epileptic fits are going to happen and take effective remedial measures to protect their owners. According to eyewitness reports, elephants screamed and ran for higher ground just before the 2004 tsunami struck India and Sri Lanka. In his book *The Hidden Life of Trees*, forester Peter Wohlleben shows how trees *know* how to communicate and look after each other.

Human infants are born with natural intelligence; they know how to breathe and how to find the breast. Adult humans can feel it too, but it is usually buried deep down below mountains of erroneous subconscious conditioning, and most of us need to have our cages rattled to realize it. Mountaineering is but one form of cage-rattling.

11

Parkinson's Disease

I WAS PROBABLY BORN WORRYING.

I came out of architecture school in 1970, aged 25, with an ulcer, probably caused by too much worrying about the world. On a 1990 Himalayan expedition, I was diagnosed with high blood pressure by the Indian doctor at base camp and advised to return home ASAP.

In 2009, I suffered a dissected aorta and was very lucky to have survived the emergency air-ambulance evacuation to Victoria and the subsequent open-heart surgery. They had to close my circulatory system down completely for eight hours while they replaced my aorta. I bounced back to good health remarkably quickly and seemed to have come away relatively unscathed.

Two years later, however, I developed a seemingly innocent and quite common condition known as "dropped foot." An MRI showed two centimetres of dead nerve tissue in my spine. A neurologist diagnosed a "spinal stroke."

"Was that," I asked, "anything to do with the eight hours without any circulation of blood and oxygen in my body and brain during my aorta surgery?"

"No. Nothing to do with it. Pure random chance."

"Humgh."

Four years later, during a consultation with the same neurologist, he asked a whole bunch of seemingly unrelated questions such as, "How's your handwriting?"

"It's all squiggly."

"How's your sense of smell?"

"Non-existent. It's completely gone!"

"I've got bad news and good news. The bad news is you've got Parkinson's disease. The good news is I can give you medication that will somewhat hold off the progression for up to five years. After that, I can't promise anything."

"Well, hell! That's three very serious medical afflictions in six years. Is the Parkinson's disease related to my aorta replacement six years ago and my spinal stroke four years ago?"

"No. You have been exceptionally unlucky. They are all completely unrelated."

"That's weird!"

....

After the Parkinson's disease (PD) diagnosis I dutifully took the prescribed heavy-duty medication – levodopa, one of the so-called "wonder drugs" of the twentieth century – but I also started reading.

PD was originally referred to as "shaking palsy" because of the signature symptom of shaking. Not all people with PD have the shakes (I don't), but there is a wide spectrum of other symptoms, of which I have about a dozen. The most obvious are impaired balance, stooped posture, loss of smell, squiggly handwriting, dragging my right foot and not swinging my right arm.

PD causes depletion of the supply of dopamine to the basal ganglia (BG), the area of the brain that governs autonomous movement. Dopamine is a neurotransmitter that delivers messages from the control centre of the brain (the frontal cortex) to the BG. Less dopamine arriving in the BG means less control of automatic, habitual, subconscious muscular activity.

Dopamine is also a "feel-good" hormone that keeps us motivated and lets us enjoy what we really like. It motivates us to take action toward goals, desires and needs and gives us a surge of reinforcing pleasure when we achieve them. Activities that give us pleasure stimulate dopamine. Procrastination, self-doubt and lack of enthusiasm are linked with low levels of dopamine. Proper muscular function and well-being requires the right balance of dopamine supply to the BG. Because it depletes that supply, PD creates a vicious circle of decline in both physical and emotional function.

Mainstream medical treatment is mainly limited to levodopa medication, but physical and mental exercise are now known to be beneficial for the treatment of PD. I take my levodopa dutifully every four hours, as prescribed, and take a 20-minute walk over rough ground every day. The limitation of the effectiveness of levodopa, especially after five years, is that the supply of dopamine can be administered only intermittently, but the demand is constant, especially in the later stages.

The medical profession now admits that the placebo effect can also help with PD, and some very interesting research supports what Bernie Siegel claimed in his 1986 book *Love, Medicine and Miracles*: that patients have significantly better chances of getting better if they *believe* they will. He also found that positive-minded patients supported by loving relationships were likelier to love themselves and work collaboratively with their doctors to self-heal.

This assertion of the healing power of love, or "mind over matter," was one of the first expressions of the new, holistic view of the world. It was very hard for the medical profession to take at the time, firmly entrenched as it was (and still is, to a large extent) in the old, mechanistic view of the world – witness my neurologist. The evidence, however, has since suggested that the placebo effect, with its associated psychological factor of feeling good about ourselves, can help deliver an uninterrupted supply of dopamine to the BG.

After the near-death experience of my aorta surgery, people asked me whether or not I saw any "bright lights," suggesting the possibility of some transformational insight. I said, "No, but I did have a renewed belief in the power of love." The number of well-wishing phone calls, emails, cards and visits I received was surprising. I had no idea people cared about me so much. There's no doubt in my mind that this, along with the incredible care of the Canadian rescue and health care system, and the loving support from family, friends and community, had a lot to do with my survival of and initial recovery from this horrendous ordeal. I did not exactly see any bright lights, but nor can I believe that my survival, which everyone agrees was extraordinary, was just a matter of luck or random chance. I'm sure there's a lot more to it than that.

Another PD management tool in my kit is "neuroplasticity" – the ability of the brain to heal itself. Conscious attention and intention can redirect messages around damaged areas, enabling the brain to repair itself. I believe this explains how I am able to alleviate some of my PD symptoms simply by focusing my conscious intention.

It seems to me that these three components of the placebo effect – focus of conscious attention; patients' participation in influencing their own recovery; the healing power of love – are also the main ingredients of the Zone. So, even as I take my medications and exercise, I am a strong advocate for the healing power of the Zone – if not for total recovery, at least for holding PD's advancement somewhat at bay. But as with levodopa, one big limitation of the effectiveness of neuroplasticity and being in the Zone is that they depend on an uninterrupted supply of conscious attention, and that is very hard to sustain.

I do also have to acknowledge the opposite of placebo: nocebo, the common and sometimes deeply embedded belief that a person will not get better. The hardest part of accessing the Zone, and being fully present in the moment, is getting rid of the subconsciously conditioned thoughts and beliefs that prevent it.

Yesterday, I fell down the stairs because I was not paying attention. A month ago, I bit my tongue because I was still in the habit of talking with my mouth full of food. Last year, I failed a driving test because I did not notice a red light. I was instructed to turn left at a four-lane intersection with no other traffic in sight and a green light for traffic proceeding straight through. But my attention was so focused on whether or not my right (injured) foot was on the brake or the gas pedal that I failed to notice the small left-turn signal, which was red. When I was given the opportunity to retake the test, I passed with no trouble.

I have not stopped worrying about the world, which is what I believe started this whole epic saga in the first place. In fact, there is more to worry about now than ever. What sane person wouldn't worry about the world? I take my blood pressure medication just as diligently as my levodopa, but I also practise being in the Zone more often and for longer periods because that, I believe, is my most effective protection against what I refer to as my "old age on steroids syndrome." That and stroking Smokey, my super-affectionate cat, who is teaching me unconditional love.

Plus I am on a waiting list for surgery for arthritis in my knee. Especially since reading about the famous experiment that showed placebo to be just as effective as surgery in healing arthritis, I can also alleviate the pain by applying the Zone principle, but once again I confess it is very difficult to sustain focused attention on more than one issue at a time. Whereas I can alleviate some of my symptoms for brief moments, sustaining that attention more often and for longer periods requires constant discipline and mental effort, which is very tiring, often boring and sometimes antisocial, if not impossible. At such moments, I have to remind myself of being on El Capitan with Mick Burke. There – in spite of, and maybe because of, horrendous adversity and even apparent "impossibility" – being in the Zone allowed me to extend my limits of possibility. Anything is possible if we put our mind to it – or, more precisely, almost anything is possible if we put a universal mind to it.

After my research, and contrary to the mechanistic belief held by the neurologist – but not so much by my GP, thankfully – I have come to the holistic conclusion that everything, including my three serious medical conditions, is related. My subconsciously induced propensity for worrying caused systemic high blood pressure, which in turn caused my aorta dissection. Lack of blood supply to my brain during my aorta surgery caused damage that was a possible cause of my PD.

12

The Zone in the Built Environment

DURING MY TRAINING AS AN ARCHITECT IN THE sixties, I developed a distaste for most "modern" architecture and a corresponding preference for "vernacular" architecture, the building language of the people. I noticed that many old buildings in the world are popular because they possess a welcoming ambience that resonates with our minds, bodies and emotions, making us feel good, whereas most modern buildings do not. On the contrary, they are often soulless and, if anything, induce negative emotional responses because they were planned, built, paid for and used by people whose mechanistic world view did not acknowledge the validity of subjective feelings.

When it was time for me to present my thesis, I encountered a serious stumbling block because at my school, and likely at any other academic institution at that time, expression of subjective "feelings" was strictly taboo. I faced the possibility of being ridiculed and dismissed as "Romantic," as in, "Poor Rob. He's such a Romantic!" The implication being that I was missing a few screws and incapable of accepting the practicality of the contemporary approach.

Inspired by the recently published Club of Rome report *The Limits to Growth*, I submitted a thesis advocating villages, instead of cities, as the ideal form of human settlement, in which the building vernacular was an expression of the lifestyle of people grounded in their surrounding natural environment. I was lucky. The thesis was accepted by the school jury, but with a proviso from the chairman, an architect famous for designing super-high-tech space colonies: "Well then, Rob, you are just going to have to get out there and build your villages, aren't you!"

So, 50 years later, here I am, living in a boat-based village, attempting to put into practice in the constructed human environment a holistic state of mind conducive to an enlightened decision-making process I learned in the wild natural environment: the Zone.

Specifically, my mission has become to facilitate organic design from the ground up with an owner/designer/builder team process that incorporates shared feelings of connectivity with the surrounding natural environment and with each other to procure unity and harmony in the whole energy field of a building and its surroundings.

I am encouraged in this by architect Chris Alexander, whose masterwork, *The Nature of Order*, applies theories of contemporary physics and biology to the design process. Alexander's approach starts with acknowledging that we do not live in a world of inert, impersonal, separate objects; instead, our world consists of vibrating energy fields whose different frequencies, like music, affect our emotions and feelings. Consequently, I have learned to pay particular attention to feeling how the relationships between the various internal and external spaces of a building contribute to and reflect the order of the whole.

I also believe that buildings look and feel best when they express synergistic input and feedback from everyone involved, so that the design takes on a life of its own as it evolves and grows. This is what I like to call "organic, soulful" architecture.

Hi, Rob,

We are an elderly couple who have recently purchased a beautiful piece of waterfront property on one of the Outer Islands and would like to build a retirement home. Our preferred general location is on a quite rugged rocky bluff sloping down to a natural beach with splendid southeast views to the ocean. We have a driveway through our property from the rear.

We had a builder from town take a look at the site and run us through some possible scenarios and costs. He explained how challenging and costly it would be to build a house on such an undulating, complex and remote site. He would likely have to blast some rock away to flatten it.

We did not like the sound of that, as we were quite sure that it would be ugly and therefore detract from the natural integrity of the site, as well as the value of the property. We feel very strongly that we want our new home, as far as possible, to enhance both the beauty and value of the property. If necessary, we could find a more practical house site elsewhere on the property rather than compromise that beautiful, pristine site on the waterfront.

Chatting with some of our new neighbours and expressing our frustration, we heard your name mentioned as a local designer who has a good reputation for helping clients design buildings that look and feel like they belong on their site. They also mentioned that you may be able to recommend a local builder to work with us as a team to help keep costs under control. We would very much appreciate you getting in touch with us to arrange a time to visit us at our site to have a chat about our project.

....

This letter is a typical first step of numerous projects I have worked on over the years. Also typical is chatting over drinks at the housewarming celebration, with the clients telling me they are pleased with the final product. When they ask if *I* am pleased with it, my answer is invariably the same: "Yes. I am pleased with the feel of the house, but I am even more pleased that you are pleased."

"Ha, ha! That sounds like a businessman talking!"

"No, that never could be," I answer. "But it *is* my philosophy."

So I showed up at the site and met the folks who had written to me, and I was able to see at a glance that the adverse, rugged complexity of the site could easily be converted into a positive generator of unique character and life in the design of the building. The superb view was to the southeast, but the site was also exposed to the prevailing wind, which could be ferocious at times – but that too could generate unique design parameters. Another positive feature of the site was the proximal stand of mature second-growth fir on the landward side, some of which would need to be felled for the driveway and possible garden site and could then be milled into timbers for the primary structure of the house.

The couple showed me some sketches of what they would like, which right away indicated their personalities. In a reversal of traditional gender stereotypes, she was energetic, analytical and systematic, whereas he was very reserved, intuitive and imaginative. I explained my preferred role as a facilitator of an organic team process in which the design would eventually evolve with a life of its own. I suggested they choose a builder right away: not only would he know current materials and local transportation costs; he would quite likely have valuable ideas, and it was important for those to be incorporated in the evolution of the design so that he would have a psychological share in its ownership. This also helped to ensure that the design could continue to evolve organically with step-by-step transformation right through the construction. To this end, I explained how important it was to have a builder they could trust. Very fortunately, we have just such a person right here on the island, and they had no trouble accepting my recommendation.

Analyzing the site's fixed features on a scale map, we began to get some idea of the location, size and shape of the house's footprint. This opportunity to do real work together on the ground was welcomed by all, especially the wife, because it involved a lot of tangible measurement and calculation.

Next morning, just when we thought we had all agreed on a final location and were ready to move ahead to the next stage, the rest of us were surprised when the husband quite vehemently proclaimed that he thought that we needed to move the building ten feet over.

"Why?" we gasped. "What the hell for?"

"Last night after our work, I was just sitting on that rock over there, chewing things over, when I realized that one of the fixed features that we had left enough comfortable allowance to avoid was the existing shack that we were actually planning to remove."

The normally reserved husband again surprised us all by proclaiming, "I knew there was a missing piece in this whole three-dimensional jigsaw puzzle. I need a hideaway. A nook."

"You've got it, love, in the attic," his wife said with a laugh.

I was very pleased with this turn of events because it demonstrated a key component of an organic, life-inducing process: the team working together with feedback loops and step-by-step transformations, not moving ahead to the next step until the effect of what had been done so far was felt and assessed. If it did not *feel* right, then we should fix it right now before it was too late.

One stinking hot early afternoon in July, the normally calm, steadfast builder was busy sawing an intricate cut on the end of the house's primary beam. Suddenly he exploded, swearing and cursing. He had just realized he had set the saw at the wrong angle, and he was mad at himself because he feared the whole beam was ruined and would be hard, if not impossible, to replace. I was able to calm him down a bit by explaining that although the angle of that cut was a pattern for all the other exposed timbers in the house, it was a purely ornamental feature, not affecting the structural function of the beams. The difference was subtle, and the subsequent cuts could all be adjusted to suit the angle of the cut he had made. The design could adapt to the feedback from the situation. It was a live process.

The project was successfully completed on schedule and on budget. The house belongs on the site. The project employed quite a few local people and was a boost to the local economy. The neighbours commented on what a good feeling the property has. The clients are happy, and we are all the best of friends. I like to think it is an example of how the holistic world view makes being in the Zone normal as opposed to extraordinary.

....

It is no doubt easier to access the Zone in deep wilderness, where there are few societal distractions, or in extreme life-threatening circumstances, but is it accessible in the artificial environment of everyday urban life?

To the extent that the Zone involves being in tune with intelligent vibrations in the natural environment – which are considered abnormal under the mechanistic world view and therefore denied and excluded – I would say definitely not. Fortunately, however, not all of everyday life, even in the city, is artificial, and the holistic world view is found even there. But holism and the Zone are likelier to flourish in rural environments, which is a good reason for preserving as much public green space as possible and maintaining an unbiased, open state of mind. The very essence of the Zone is expanding the boundaries of possibility, which gives some grounds for hope. Whether we realize it or not, we create our own reality, so why not choose to create a harmonious, loving and sustainable reality instead of a sterile, hateful, self-destructive one? To all appearances, sadly, adherents of the holistic view are fighting a losing battle in the rapidly expanding cities of today.

13

The Future of the Collective Zone

AS WE SAW IN CHAPTER 10, CONTEMPORARY SOCI-ety's systematic disconnection from nature's intelligent order is also a disconnection from what is real, and from the critical path of survival. Climbing mountains was (and still is, in that living with old age and PD is now a metaphorical mountain) my deliberate, conscious attempt to reconnect with the spontaneous flow of nature's intelligent order. Even though I like to believe that my understanding aligns with traditional mountaineering values shared by many of my peers in our time, I realize I cannot claim be a spokesperson for any values other than my own. And climbing the mountain is not by any means the only way of rattling the subconscious cage, extending the limits of possibility and getting into the Zone. There are many others.

Society is fast losing the window of opportunity to avert global climate conditions dramatically unfavourable to human life. It faces an onslaught of propaganda from vested interests promoting the mechanistic world view, reducing the meaning of intelligence to be mere cognitive ability, and engendering the dangerous, potentially self-fulfilling prophecy that we will become computing machines, lacking human feelings (love) and the vitality and diversity of life necessary for survival.

Perhaps the most significant and consequential mistake myth of a single-mindedly mechanistic world view of the world is the belief that ever-increasing material wealth is the only way to achieve meaningful happiness. The Zone has the potential to provide a more honest, effective and far less destructive source of happiness than material aggrandizement. This is especially true if you can avoid mortgages and debt. The means and extent to which Laurie and I have achieved sustained happiness without mortgages or debt – despite myriad setbacks – is, I believe, the most significant aspect of our lifestyle that I would hope might inspire people trying to break out of the conditioned mechanistic cage and rediscover their natural self.

My humble opinion is not that the old, mechanistic approach supported by logic and reason (Descartes's "I think, therefore I am") is inherently wrong. What is wrong is the adamant belief that it is the *only* valid world view. That belief excludes any understanding of reality supported by other forms of natural intelligence, such as imagination, intuition, memory and ethics, or by personal feelings, which are more concerned with the relationships between things, the wave aspect of reality. Holistic understanding is not exclusive but a combination, a dynamic balance of the particle and wave aspects of reality. "I think *and feel*, therefore I am."

....

If humanity, in any form resembling existing civilization, is to survive the imminent tumultuous changes to the earth's climate that our own greed and exponential growth have created, the holistic, natural Zone state of mind will have to prevail, whether by choice or by having nature thrust it upon us. Unlike its mechanistic counterpart, it has eons of evolutionary intelligence inherent in it.

I am reminded of James Lovelock's theory that life on earth functions as if it were a single living organism, self-regulating to create the conditions most favourable to sustaining life. In his 1979 book *Gaia: A New Look at Life on Earth*, he wrote:

"The evolution of homo sapiens, with his technological inventiveness and his increasingly subtle communications network, has vastly increased Gaia's range of perception. She is now, through us, awake and aware of herself. She has seen the reflection of her fair face through the eyes of astronauts and television cameras of orbiting spacecraft. Our sensations of wonder and pleasure, our capacity for conscious thought and speculation, and our endless curiosity and drive are hers to share. This new interrelationship of Gaia with man is by no means fully established; we are not yet a truly collective species, corralled and tamed as an integral part of the biosphere, as we are as individual creatures. It may be that the destiny of mankind is to become tamed, so that the fierce, destructive, and greedy forces of tribalism and nationalism are fused into a compulsive urge to belong to the commonwealth of creatures which constitutes Gaia. It might seem to be a surrender, but I suspect that the rewards, in the form of an increased sense of wellbeing and fulfillment, in knowing ourselves to be a dynamic part of a far greater entity, would be worth the loss of tribal freedom."

....

As I write this, in the spring of 2020, in view of society's spectacular failure to start making the lifestyle changes necessary to avert catastrophic climate change, nature, in the form of the coronavirus pandemic, is forcing those exact changes upon us, with deadly precision. After the virus has run its course, a worst-case long-term scenario would be for human society to return to its old, mechanistic, delinquent business as usual, having learned absolutely nothing, and continue fighting about which fictional order has the right and capability to control the world, provoking no doubt even more devastating and deadly responses from nature – Gaia's revenge.

Or, at best, might we hope that the suffering unleashed by the coronavirus will serve as a collective wake-up call. Then, like climbers entering the Zone in a fierce mountain storm, we might tune into and participate in the very real, infinitely wonderful, spontaneously evolving flow of Nature's universal intelligence. We might allow it to guide our behaviour, to find the most appropriate adaptive response. And then we will rediscover what is real and who we are.

....

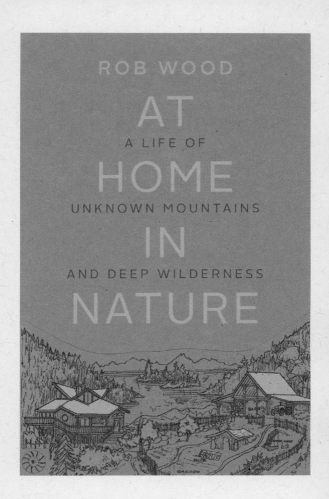

At Home in Nature: A Life of
Unknown Mountains and Deep Wilderness
ISBN 9781771602501

Rob Wood grew up in a village on the edge of the Yorkshire Moors, where he eventually developed a preoccupation with rock climbing. After studying architecture for five years at the Architectural Association School in London, England, he made his way to Montreal and ended up in Calgary. During his time in Calgary, Rob became a pioneer of ice climbing and posted numerous first ascents in the Rockies during the early 1970s.

Eventually, life in corporate Alberta proved unfulfilling and Rob realized that he needed to find a place where he could reconnect with nature, which brought him to the remote reaches of Canada's West Coast. Settling on Maurelle Island, he and his wife built an off-the-grid homestead and focussed on alternative communities and developing a small house-design practice specializing in organic and wholesome building techniques.

At Home in Nature is a gentle and philosophical memoir that focuses on living a life deeply rooted in the natural world, where citizens are connected to the planet and individuals work together to help, enhance and make the world a better — and sustainable — place.